leapfrog
Learners

Big Cats

by Annabelle Lynch

W
FRANKLIN WATTS
LONDON • SYDNEY

First published in 2012 by
Franklin Watts
338 Euston Road
London
NW1 3BH

Franklin Watts Australia
Level 17/207 Kent Street
Sydney
NSW 2000

Picture credits: Shutterstock: front cover,
1, 8, 5, 10-11, 12, 15, 19 ;
Peter Malmsbury.iStockphoto: 7; Richard du
Troit/Minden Pictures/FLPA: 16-17; Yojik/
Dreamstime: 20.

A CIP catalogue record for this book is
available from the British Library.

Dewey number: 599.7'55

ISBN 978 1 4451 0322 8 (hbk)
ISBN 978 1 4451 0330 3 (pbk)

Series Editor: Melanie Palmer
Picture Researcher: Diana Morris
Series Advisor: Catherine Glavina
Series Designer: Peter Scoulding

Printed in China

Franklin Watts is a division of Hachette Children's Books,
an Hachette UK company. www.hachette.co.uk

Contents

What are big cats?   4

In the grasslands   6

In the jungle   8

Fast cats   10

Finding food   12

Big cat senses   14

Big cat babies   16

In danger   18

Big cats and small cats   20

Glossary   22

Quiz   23

Answers and Index   24

The words in **bold** can be found in the glossary.

What are big cats?

Big cats are large cats that live in the **wild**. They are much bigger than pet cats!

Lions have a very loud roar!

In the grasslands

Lions, cheetahs and leopards live in **grasslands** around the world.

Can you find grassland areas on a map?

In the jungle

Tigers live in **jungles** and forests. Their colours make it easy for them to hide.

9

A tiger can creep up without beeing seen.

Fast cats

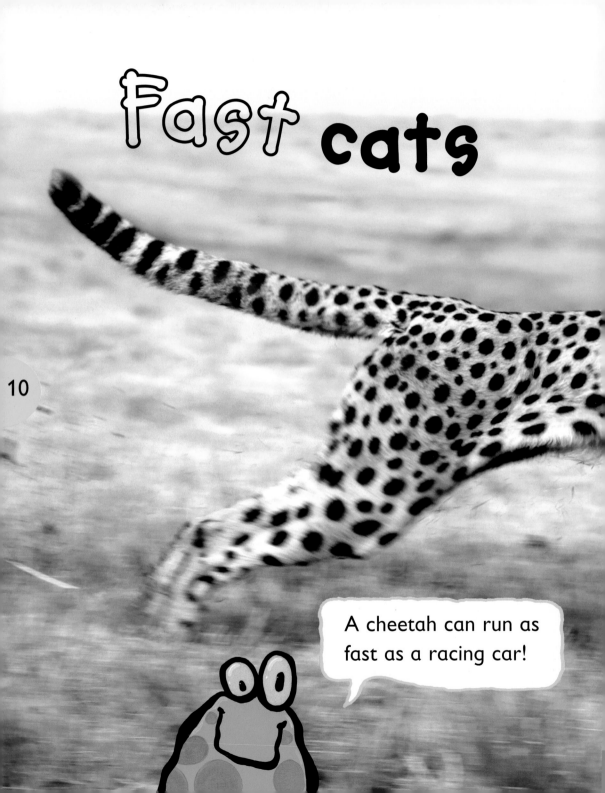

A cheetah can run as fast as a racing car!

Big cats can run fast.
Cheetahs are the fastest
animals on dry land!

Finding food

All big cats eat
meat. They **hunt**
and chase other
animals.

Female lions do more
hunting than male lions.

Big cat senses

All big cats have good hearing and eyesight, and can move quickly.

Jaguars have smooth fur and long whiskers.

Big cat babies

Cubs often learn to hunt in packs.

Big cats have babies called cubs. They feed their cubs milk until the cubs learn to hunt.

In danger

Today there are fewer big cats in the wild. People have killed them for their **fur**.

How can we help look after big cats like this snow leaopard?

Big cat and small cats

Pet cats come from the same animal group as big cats.

Pet cats can't roar. What sound do they make?

Glossary

Grassland - area of flat, dry land

Hunt - find and kill animals

Jungle - area of land full of plants

Prey - an animal that is hunted and eaten

Wild - living in its natural environment

Websites:

http://animals.nationalgeographic.com/animals/
http://www.pluspets.net/facts-big-cats/
http://www.sciencekids.co.nz/sciencefacts/animals.
html

Every effort has been made by the Publishers to ensure that the websites are suitable for children, and that they contain no inappropriate or offensive material. However, because of the nature of the Internet, it is impossible to guarantee that the contents of these sites will not be altered. We strongly advise that Internet access is supervised by a responsible adult.

Quiz

1. What do you call baby big cats ?

2. What do big cats eat?

3. Which cat is the fastest animal on land?

4. Why do tigers have stripes?

5. What are big cats hunted for?

6. What do cubs feed on?

The answers are on page 24

Answers

1. Cubs
2. Meat from other animals
3. The cheetah
4. So they can hunt without being seen
5. Their fur
6. Milk

Index

Cheetah 6-7, 10-11

Cub 16-17

Grassland 6

Hunt 12

Jaguar 14-15

Jungle 9

Leopard 16-17

Lion 4-5,

Pet cats 18-19

Tiger 8-9

Wild 4